# WOMEN OF MYTHOLOGY
## GODDESSES, WARRIORS, AND HUNTERS

# PALLAS ATHENA

Laura L. Sullivan

Cavendish Square
New York

Published in 2020 by Cavendish Square Publishing, LLC
243 5th Avenue, Suite 136, New York, NY 10016

Copyright © 2020 by Cavendish Square Publishing, LLC

First Edition

Library of Congress Cataloging-in-Publication Data

Names: Sullivan, Laura L., 1974- author.
Title: Pallas Athena / Laura L. Sullivan.
Description: New York : Cavendish Square, 2020. | Series: Women of mythology: goddesses, warriors, and hunters | Includes bibliographical references and index.
Identifiers: LCCN 2019008841 (print) | LCCN 2019009672 (ebook) |
ISBN 9781502651396 (ebook) | ISBN 9781502651389 (library bound) |
ISBN 9781502651365 (pbk.) | ISBN 9781502651372 (6 pack)
Subjects: LCSH: Athena (Greek deity)--Juvenile literature. | Mythology, Greek--Juvenile literature.
Classification: LCC BL820.M6 (ebook) | LCC BL820.M6 S85 2020 (print) | DDC 292.2/114--dc23
LC record available at https://lccn.loc.gov/2019008841

Editor: Kristen Susienka
Copy Editor: Alex Tessman
Associate Art Director: Alan Sliwinski
Designer: Christina Shults
Production Coordinator: Karol Szymczuk
Photo Research: J8 Media

Printed in the United States of America

# TABLE OF CONTENTS

Athena is remembered in Greece today. This Athena statue is at the Academy of the Arts in Greece.

# CHAPTER ONE
# ATHENA THE WISE

**P**allas Athena was a goddess in ancient Greece. Most people know her by the name Athena.

The Greeks had many different gods and goddesses. Each god or goddess was in charge of certain things. Athena was the goddess of wisdom, war, and crafts like **weaving**.

# The Birth of Athena

In Greek myths, Athena was the daughter of Zeus. He ruled the gods. Her mother was Metis. She was the goddess of tricks and being smart. Zeus was afraid Metis would have a child who was smarter than he was, so he turned Metis into a fly. Then, he swallowed her. After that, she lived in his head. Inside Zeus's head, Metis gave birth to their daughter Athena.

This gave Zeus a terrible headache. One of the other gods split his skull open. Out jumped Athena. She was an adult. She wore armor, or a suit of metal.

# HESIOD

Hesiod wrote about gods and myths. He lived some time between 750 and 650 BCE. He wrote a lot. One poem he wrote was called *Theogony*. It was about the beginnings of the Greek gods. He wrote about Athena being born from Zeus's head. He also tells a story about the creation of the earth, sky, oceans, and universe. Hesiod told these stories in poem form.

This sculpture imagines what Hesiod looked like.

Artwork on an ancient pot shows Athena being born as an adult from Zeus's head.

## Athena's Best Friend

Athena had a mortal, or human, foster sister named Pallas. They were both warriors, or fighters. Pallas was Athena's best friend. One day, they were showing off their skills with a spear. It was just practice. No one was supposed to get hurt. However, when

Pallas was winning, Zeus was upset. He distracted Pallas when she should have blocked Athena's spear. Athena accidentally killed her best friend. After that, Athena adopted Pallas's name to honor her. The goddess became Pallas Athena.

## Clever Athena

Athena was a very clever goddess. Both she and Poseidon, the god of the sea, wanted

### Myth, Fable, or Folktale?

Myths, fables, and folklore are similar but have important differences. A myth is a story that often has a god or gods in it. A fable tells a moral or lesson. It often includes animals. Folklore stories, or folktales, entertain listeners and readers. They were passed on by common people.

# ANOTHER STORY: GODS AND PRIDE

In myths, gods have human emotions, like jealousy and anger. Pride is one strong emotion.

Pride means being satisfied with yourself. To the ancient Greeks, pride could be a bad thing. A kind of pride called **hubris** was very bad. People with hubris thought they were better than everyone—even the gods. Athena hated hubris. She would punish people who thought they were better than her.

Gods in other cultures didn't like things that tried to be better than them either. Inanna was a goddess in Mesopotamia, in the Middle East. She was a goddess of war, government, love, and beauty. One day she saw Ehbi, a mountain. Inanna was angry that the mountain dared to be so big and beautiful. She thought it was trying to be better than her. So she smashed it to dust.

Pallas was young Athena's best friend and foster sister.

to be the god of the city of Athens. They had a contest to see who could give the city the best gift. Poseidon hit the rocks with his **trident** and made a spring, but the spring was salty. Athena made an olive tree. It gave the people food, wood, and oil. Athena was the winner. Athens became her city.

The Greeks believed the gods lived on Mount Olympus.

# CHAPTER TWO
# ATHENA BRINGS ORDER

The ancient Greeks had a myth about how the universe began. At first, there was no earth or sky. There was just confusion. Nothing had shape. That place was called Chaos. Later, the gods like Athena created order out of chaos. Greek people believed the gods made laws. They created people and animals. They gave the world structure.

Greek civilization began in a similar way. Early on, there were only separate villages and small cities. There was no unity. Each city had its own gods and goddesses. Later, Greece began to come together as one civilization. There were big areas like Athens and Sparta. At the same time, all parts of Greece began to believe in the same gods. The gods gave civilization structure.

## Two War Gods

The gods and goddesses represented things the Greeks needed to be strong and unified, or one group. Athena wasn't just a goddess of war. She was a goddess of *smart* warfare. Her brother Ares was the

Athena's brother Ares was the god of bloody fighting and war.

god of crazy, violent, bloody war. Athena liked cleverness and planning. She was the goddess who used war to create big **empires**. Ares just loved to fight.

## Democracy

The Greeks invented **democracy**. That is a government where citizens vote for their leaders. Democracy began in Athens. Athena was the goddess of Athens. The values she stood for became important to the city. Her wisdom helped the city grow. People in Athens looked to her example to run their city well. Later, democracy spread to other Greek cities. Soon, all free men could vote.

## Many Goddesses

Human women in most of ancient Greece didn't have a lot of power or rights. They were controlled by their closest male relatives. The goddesses, however, were very important and powerful.

### Roman Goddess

Minerva is the Roman version of Athena. She is also the goddess of arts, wisdom, and war.

There were many Greek goddesses. This sculpture imagines what Artemis, the goddess of hunting, looked like. She was strong and beautiful.

# WOMEN INSPIRED BY ATHENA

In ancient times, things like taking care of children, making cloth, and cooking were jobs for women. Things like politics, business, and war were for men. Athena combined both female and male things. For example, she dealt with weaving and war.

Different parts of Greece had different ideas about women. In the city of Athens, women couldn't vote or own property. They were supposed to be mothers, weavers, and housekeepers. Athena as a weaver and craftswoman was most like them. In the city of Sparta, though, women had more rights. Athena the warrior and politician was more important to them. Women in both Athens and Sparta liked Athena's cleverness and wisdom. That was useful in crafts and also in war.

There were many goddesses in Greek mythology. Artemis was the goddess of hunting. Aphrodite was goddess of love and beauty. Demeter was goddess of the plants and crops. Persephone was the goddess of the Underworld. Hera was the queen of the gods. Each goddess was just as important as the gods.

## Sappho

Sappho (630–570 BCE) was a female poet who wrote about love, motherhood, and the gods and goddesses. One of her poems is called "Ode to Aphrodite." It celebrates the goddess of love.

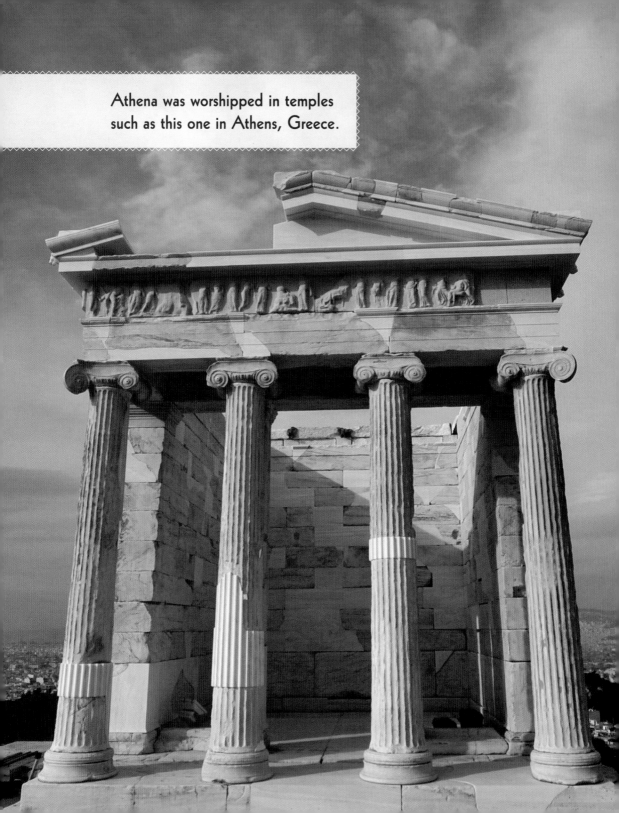

Athena was worshipped in temples such as this one in Athens, Greece.

# CHAPTER THREE
# ATHENA TODAY

Athena was a popular goddess until at least the fourth century CE. Back when people believed in her, women didn't have many rights. However, Athena showed ancient women that they could be smart and wise. They could use their skills for many things. They could do things men could do too.

Today, Athena is still a **symbol** of how powerful women can be.

## Athena in Stories

Athena and other gods and goddesses are in TV shows, books, and movies today. For example, *Percy Jackson and the Olympians* is a popular kids' book series by Rick Riordan. It has many Greek gods and goddesses in it. Athena is one of the characters in this book series.

### Athena's Owl

Owls are the symbol of Athena, goddess of wisdom. Because of this, people today still think owls are wise birds.

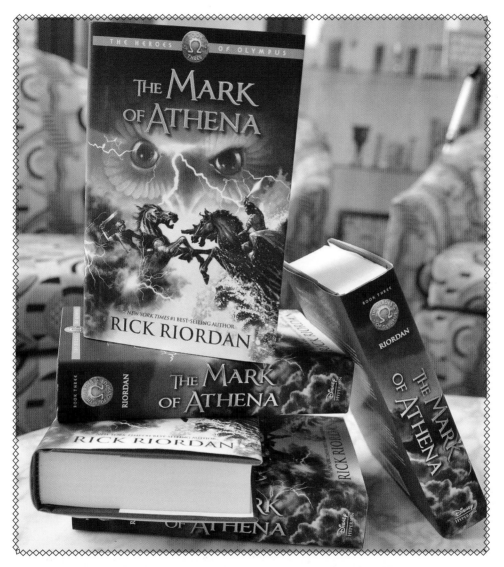

Today, Athena is a character in many movies and books, like this one by author Rick Riordan.

# Official Athena

Athena is on the state **seal** of California. When the United States started, most states began as big areas of land. They were called territories. Later, they became states. California, however, was never a territory. It skipped that part and became a state right away. The state has Athena on its seal because it started fully grown, like Athena.

The Medal of Honor is the highest award

Some say Minerva is on California's seal. Others say it's Athena.

the US military can give someone. The US Army, Navy, and Air Force have different medals. The army and navy medals show Minerva, or the Roman goddess who was like Athena. (Romans and Greeks shared a lot of the same gods, just with different names.) The army medal has just Minerva's head. The navy medal shows her forcing away a man holding snakes.

## Athena in College

At the start of each school year, students at Wells College in Aurora, New York, decorate a statue of Athena/Minerva. Near the end of their time at college, students kiss the statue's feet for good luck.

# ATHENA IN THE ARMY

This is our war...

Join the WAAC

WOMEN'S ARMY AUXILIARY CORPS
UNITED STATES ARMY

APPLY AT ANY U. S. ARMY RECRUITING AND INDUCTION STATION

This poster advertises the WAAC with Athena's image in the background.

In World War II, women could not fight, but they could join the army in the Women's Army Auxiliary Corps (WAAC). It let women work in the army as bakers, nurses, drivers, and more. These women chose Athena as their mascot. They wore an image of her on their uniforms. She appeared on posters to get more women to join the WAAC.

One day every year, past members of the WAAC have lunch together. The lunch's leader, or hostess, dresses up as Athena to make a speech. The members call their mascot "Minnie." It's short for Athena's Roman name, Minerva.

This statue of Athena stands in Guadalajara, Mexico. It shows her wearing a suit of armor and a helmet. She holds a spear and shield.

## Athena and Fun

There are two different Athena Barbie dolls.
One shows her as the armored goddess of

war. The other shows her with an owl, as the goddess of wisdom.

This is the Athena: Goddess of War Barbie.

Athena is a mascot, or symbol, of school clubs and college groups. Many universities have a statue of her. Products are named after her. There are Athena yogurt bars, Athena bottled water, and Athena makeup. If you look around, you might notice Athena in a lot more places!

# GLOSSARY

**democracy**  A kind of government where people vote for their leaders.

**empires**  Groups of territories or peoples under one ruler.

**hubris**  Too much pride.

**seal**  A drawing that goes with different cities or countries.

**symbol**  Something that stands for something else; a sign.

**trident**  A long spear with three points.

**weaving**  Making cloth by using threads made of wool or plant material.

# FIND OUT MORE

## Books

Briggs, Korwin. *Gods and Heroes: Mythology Around the World.* New York, NY: Workman, 2018.

Riordan, Rick. *Percy Jackson's Greek Gods.* New York, NY: Disney Hyperion, 2016.

## Website

**The Gods and Goddesses of Ancient Greece**

www.natgeokids.com/za/discover/history/greece/greek-gods

## Video

**The Story of Arachne**

www.youtube.com/watch?v=qW3Bbav7w4A

# INDEX

Page numbers in **boldface** refer to images. Entries in **boldface** are glossary terms.

# ABOUT THE AUTHOR

**Laura L. Sullivan** is the author of more than forty fiction and nonfiction books for children, including the fantasies *Under the Green Hill* and *Guardian of the Green Hill*. She lives in Florida where she likes to bike, hike, kayak, hunt fossils, and practice Brazilian jiujitsu. Her favorite goddess is Artemis, goddess of the wilderness, wild animals, and the moon.